# Sea Horses

by Lola M. Schaefer

Consulting Editor: Gail Saunders-Smith, Ph.D.

Consultant: Jody Byrum, Science Writer,
SeaWorld Education Department

Pebble Books

an imprint of Capstone Press
Mankato, Minnesota

Pebble Books are published by Capstone Press
818 North Willow Street, Mankato, Minnesota 56001
http://www.capstone-press.com

*Library of Congress Cataloging-in-Publication Data*
Schaefer, Lola M., 1950–
    Sea horses/by Lola M. Schaefer.
      p. cm.—(Ocean life)
    Includes bibliographical references and index.
    Summary: In simple text and illustrations, describes the sea horse.
    ISBN 0-7368-0249-5
    1. Sea horses—Juvenile literature. [1. Sea horses.] I. Title. II. Series: Schaefer,
Lola M., 1950–    Ocean life.
QL638.S9S34         1999
597'.6798—dc21                                                        98-46078
                                                                           CIP
                                                                            AC

J
597.6798
SCH
c. 1

$13.25

## Note to Parents and Teachers

The Ocean Life series supports national science standards for units
on the diversity and unity of life. The series shows that animals
have features that help them live in different environments. This
book describes and illustrates sea horses, their appearance, and
their life cycle. The photographs support emergent readers in
understanding the text. The repetition of words and phrases helps
emergent readers learn new words. This book also introduces
emergent readers to subject-specific vocabulary words, which are
defined in the Words to Know section. Emergent readers may need
assistance to read some words and to use the Table of Contents,
Words to Know, Read More, Internet Sites, and Index/Word List
sections of the book.

2

# Table of Contents

Sea Horses . . . . . . . . . . . . . . . 5

Appearance . . . . . . . . . . . . . . 9

Eggs and Young . . . . . . . . . . 17

Note to Parents and Teachers . . . 2

Words to Know . . . . . . . . . 22

Read More . . . . . . . . . . . 23

Internet Sites . . . . . . . . . . . 23

Index/Word List . . . . . . . . . 24

Sea horses are fish.

fins

Sea horses use fins to swim.

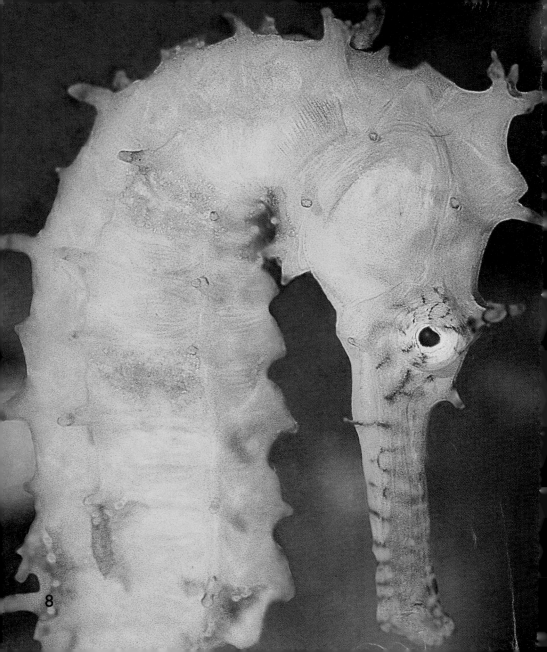

8

Sea horses have a
head that looks like
a horse head.

10

Sea horses have
a long tail.

Sea horses hold on to
seaweed with their tails.

pouch

14

Male sea horses have a pouch.

16

Female sea horses
lay eggs in the pouch.

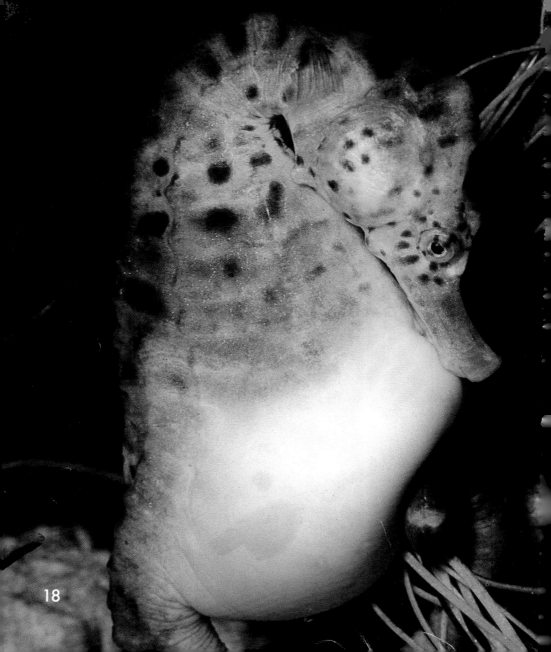

18

Male sea horses carry the eggs in the pouch.

Young sea horses hatch
and leave the pouch.

# Words to Know

**female**—an animal that can give birth or lay eggs; female sea horses lay eggs.

**fin**—a body part that a fish uses to move and steer in the water

**hatch**—to break out of an egg

**male**—an animal that can father young; male sea horses carry eggs in a pouch.

**pouch**—a pocket of skin used to carry eggs or baby animals; male sea horses carry the eggs after female sea horses lay the eggs.

**seaweed**—a plant that grows in the ocean; sea horses hide from predators in seaweed.

# Read More

**Landau, Elaine.** *Sea Horses.* A True Book. New York: Children's Press, 1999.

**Stefoff, Rebecca.** *Sea Horse.* Living Things. New York: Benchmark Books, 1997.

**Walker, Sally M.** *Sea Horses.* Minneapolis: Carolrhoda Books, 1998.

# Internet Sites

**Ask Shamu: Sea Horse**
http://www.seaworld.org/ask_shamu/seahorse.html

**Kingdom of the Seahorse**
http://www.pbs.org/wgbh/nova/seahorse/basics.html

**The Sea Horse**
http://www.icon.portland.or.us/education/vose/kidopedia/seahorse.html

# Index/Word List

eggs, 17, 19
female, 17
fins, 7
fish, 5
hatch, 21
head, 9
hold, 13
horse, 9
long, 11

looks, 9
male, 15, 19
pouch, 15, 17, 19, 21
sea horses, 5, 7, 9, 11, 13, 15, 17, 19, 21
seaweed, 13
swim, 7
tail, 11, 13
young, 21

**Word Count: 67**
**Early-Intervention Level: 8**

**Editorial Credits**
Martha E. Hillman, editor; Steve Christensen, cover designer and illustrator; Kimberly Danger and Sheri Gosewisch, photo researchers

**Photo Credits**
Art Brewer, 4
Brandon D. Cole, 10, 14
Brian Parker/Tom Stack & Associates, 8
Dembinsky Photo Assoc. Inc./Mark J. Thomas, 6
James P. Rowan, 1
Mark Conlin/Mo Yung Productions, 18
Rudie Kuiter/Innerspace Visions, 16, 20
SeaWorld, 12. Copyright 1998 SeaWorld, Inc. All rights reserved. Reproduced by permission.
Visuals Unlimited/K. B. Sandved, cover

AAV-7907